PALM TREES

by

Nick Twemlow

Acknowledgements: My gratitude to the editors of these publications, where some of these poems first appeared: *A Public Space, Boston Review, Court Green, Denver Quarterly, Fence, jubilat, Keep Going, Kiosk, Lit, MAKE, New American Writing, Northwest Review, Seattle Review, Sentence, Tammy, Volt*, and *Zoland Poetry Anthology.* ¶ "I Love Karate" was reprinted in *Best American Nonrequired Reading, 2009* (Mariner Books). ¶ Some of these poems appeared in the chapbook, *Your Mouth is Everywhere* (Racquetball Tournament Press, 2010). Thanks to Nick Demske. ¶ "Foreign Affairs" appeared in *The City Visible: Chicago Poetry for the New Century* (Cracked Slab Books, 2007). ¶ There are many who endured the various iterations of Twemlow over the life of this book. My love to all of you: Erica Bernheim, Eula Biss, John Bresland, Suzanne Buffam, Andy Carter, Ryan Dawley, Josh Edwards, my family—Lee, Megan, Sarah, Steve, Mum, Dad, Susan, and Sacha—Andrew Feld, Robert Fernandez, Jorie Graham, Brian Harty, Mary Hickman, August Kleinzahler, Kevin Larimer, Tod Marshall, Josh May, Ray Nolan, Srikanth Reddy, Fred Sasaki, Ben Sparks, David Trinidad, Pimone Triplett, and Lynn Xu. ¶ I am grateful to the Fulbright Foundation; Bill Manhire and the International Institute of Modern Letters, Victoria University, Wellington, New Zealand; and the Brown Foundation Fellows Program at the Dora Maar Residence for support during the completion of this book.

First printing 2012
Edition of 500
Special edition of 125 with screen print covers

ISBN 978-0-9884185-1-6

Published by Green Lantern Press
1511 N Milwaukee Avenue, Second Floor, Chicago, IL 60622
www.press.thegreenlantern.org

Screen printed cover art, cover, and page design by Sonnenzimmer
Typeset in Alright Sans, Harriet
Typeface design by The Okay Type Foundry, Chicago, IL
Interior paper: Finch Natural
Printed by Book Mobile, Minneapolis, MN

For Robyn

INTRODUCTION BY ROBERT FERNANDEZ

I could use Nick Twemlow's *Palm Trees* as an occasion to say something about fearlessness and destruction in poetry, the kind of work, in line with Blake and Nietzsche, whose generous mandate is to clear away the necrosis of complacency, self-satisfaction, and delusion. I could use it as an occasion to talk about sensibility, how it is the evidence of close attention, labor, and commitment—a commitment to what one wants to defend and to the possibility of a vision and a life that seeks to elaborate not only itself but that which is other than and more than itself. But I am afraid that each would paint *Palm Trees* as either too iconoclastic or utopian, and if it is either it is only so by virtue of its immersion in the particulars of contemporary life—by virtue of being, in Rimbaud's terms, "absolutely modern," that is, capable of deftly gliding along the outlines of wherever and whenever it is that we find ourselves when we find ourselves in the contemporary. The poems of *Palm Trees* glide, but they also see and have the dexterity and speed to stall, arrest, and evaluate. Twemlow is capable of effortlessly becoming many and of simultaneously affirming and negating, asserting and second-guessing. He is at once debased and ecstatic, resigned and ambitious, victim and victimizer. Simply put, I don't think that there is today a mind that thinks in poetry the paradoxes of the contemporary quite as agilely and truthfully. He is like Pope, if Pope grew up in the late 20th-century in Topeka and had the humility to recognize that the self's bid for authenticity — not the performance of its own moral conviction or intelligence—presents the ultimate, the most anguishing and acute, of rhetorical games. Thankfully this is not just a game. Indeed, *Palm Trees* has given everything, left nothing out, held nothing back. For those who would know how to live and work in poetry courageously and with a sense of joyful abandon, this book is as much a sneer as a welcoming occasion, a gauntlet thrown down.

CONTENTS

EMINENT VICTORIANA

So I walk into the house Mies van der Rohe
designed at gunpoint, the cocaine was tiresome
by this point, but that was its attraction.
I can take anything I want because I have been filmed
fucking the richest heiress in the known world.
I would like the word you keep locked
in the safe behind the Richter in the guest bedroom.
The word for the kind of ease that you recline
into after a colonic and tonic.
Give me supersonic. I want the gardener's
daughter's virginity, the fall
of Rome and the rise
of a gangster nation. I fucked everything.
I fucked the Cornish game hen.
It was so lifeless I put a fork in its face.
I am too young to remark on death.
I hope it resembles the view
you tear open
with your toy sword, toy sword,
say it ten times fast.

BLACK HELICOPTER

Seven suns sin the sky
days fazing at great speed.
Twitch of tree branch in the periphery
miserly chronotopes, tying & untying.
Black helicopter leaves amnesiatic
wake. I had the feeling,
alone in the field,
of being watched. Over my shoulder,
it was there, black helicopter,
then it was not. I
couldn't make out any identifying marks.
A few birds hop-graph
the skeletal tree.
Jacked into song,
I make a living at elision
yoking skip-trace to icicles
for fingertips. Nothing happens
yesterday. Nothing happens beyond my cubicle,
where I write on company time.
Black helicopter arrives from nothing,
researches, departs to nothing.
This is pastoral — I walk among the sheep,
flatten against hillside when black
helicopter surges over, shadow
of black helicopter
blankets the valley, something
natural about the semaphoring
raven once trained to fly into open Soviet
windows, fly out clasping canisters
detailing Soviet plans
detailing the evolution
of avian surveillance — first raven,
then raven-sized drone marked
by imperceptible noise signature
and radar signature of the raven,

then empty canister where
black helicopter blueprint should be.

Thus the raven blots the red sky
in clutch of an earlier version of itself, itself
an early avian draft of black helicopter.

I LOVE KARATE

I love karate. I love karate so much I sweat karate steak dinners. I love karate so much I eat karate cereal in the morning, karate sandwiches for lunch, and karate haiku for pleasure. But like a good karateka (that's the technical term for highly skilled karate person) I don't eat karate dessert. You know why? Because dessert takes the edge off. You might ask, Off what? but if you do, I'll perform a random karate move on you, as I did my mother when she tried to serve me non-karate cereal, one morning. That was the morning when I realized that I was a true karateka. I refused the Empire's cereal. If you are a true karateka, you are a rogue. Rogues don't like the Empire. This means that rogues spend a lot of time building dojos in the woods. A dojo is the technical name for a rogue who spends a lot of time building cabins in the woods. There are some karate moves that I can't show you. Those are secret karate moves. Like all karate moves, they are designed to kill. But these secret strikes kill faster and harder. They are to regular karate moves what hardcore is to softcore pornography. I was sensitive once, but karate got rid of that. Now I am tough on the inside as well as the outside. For example, if I was in the Oval Office partying with the President, smoking some grass (which I'd fake doing because karatekas don't smoke grass), I'd ask him to repeat what he said about kicking evil's ass and then I'd ask him to show me how he'd do it. Since I know the President isn't a karateka, I'd administer a very secret strike on him at the moment he showed me how he'd do it. That's pretty much how I'd do things. I want karate to be in the Olympics in Beijing because I want to be on the team and travel to Beijing and win a gold medal. Or at least that's what I'd trick everyone into thinking I was doing. Part of being a good karateka means bolstering the Chinese economy. Sort of like ninjas except a karateka can beat a ninja fourteen out of ten times. So while people would think I wanted to go to Beijing to win a gold medal and hang out in the Olympic Village and have a really good time with all the other athletes and media and officials and tourists, I'd really have a secret agenda. Secret agendas are pretty common for most karatekas. Secret agendas ensure that no matter what you say, you really don't mean it. So when everyone else was having a good time at the Olympics in Beijing, seeing how Communism is really good on the citizens of China because the government rounded up, the year before, tens of thousands of homeless people and relocated them to work details in provincial labor camps, I'd slip out at night and administer random karate moves on officials of the Empire. This happened a lot in Atlanta, too, when we held the Olympics. The part about the homeless I mean.

THE TWENTY-FOUR COMPLICATIONS

The life of the party slits its wrists. Its wrists
slit their wrists. The wrist of the world
wears a Patek Philippe Henry Graves

Supercomplication. Which is not a wristwatch but a pocket
watch. Among its twenty-four complications
is one for the hour in which you hang

yourself by your wedding tie and another that counts the number
of people whose livers can no longer self-repair
and have begun to eat themselves. The man

who commissioned the piece may or may not have lived
forever. He may or may not have been part-owner
of an explosives company that may or may

not go by the name of Blackwater. You
may or may not believe this, but when I was a boy
all I wanted was to push a big red button.

Imagine a million crosshairs congregating on the last
illegal alien on earth, who resembles the shape you
clock time in front of the bathroom mirror

re-imagining. Or the clock tower you climb
as Charles Whitman did in Austin, Texas
(it was not a clock tower), lugging

a duffel of guns and a hatred of the kind of muffled
conversation he always walked into
in the rooms of the house he grew up in to hear.

Meanwhile Blackwater backpedals. Blackwater occupies
the clock tower, killing time in the peculiar way time
and money prepare you for. The thesis

statement is that privatizing the military
privatizes the boredom of observing
an alien people who busy themselves

with the rituals of the free market. Learn
from the example of the markets in Jerusalem.
The seventh complication

is a koan wrapped in an enigma. What are you doing?
We're innovating.
How?

We haven't ideated that yet. Eight resembles the head
of an amber fish, the body ripped away
by a motherless shark. Nine accrues interest

in the leper colonies of the imagination
(which may or may not exist, lyrically).
Ten through seventeen take a few

bongers while watching *The Wire* on DVD. Eighteen
is your father's will,
which faded as the years passed

while burning a hole in his afterlife as the lawyers recited
its damages to your family ten days after he poked
a hole in the sky with his third eye, which, technically,

is the eighteenth complication.
Nineteen is the dream in which you marveled
at a child's Art Deco sand castle

while the lion paced a few feet away.
Twenty was last century.
Twenty-one occupies the analytic couch

your father fashioned out of chocolate glazed donuts. The next
two slob the knob of the infinite
40oz, dreaming in daiquiri, screaming

to the open field in a Whitmanic mania.
Twenty-fourth complication
of the Patek Philippe Henry Graves

Supercomplication is the server space of your next
ten years, where dust compiles and Blackwater
offloads the epic we all had hoped one of us would write.

TOPEKA, TOPEKA

Topeka, half the moon is rotten with shadows pooling in the Sea of Topeka.
Topeka, where first I wet my brain with a 40oz bottle of Topeka.
Topeka, is place name, is damn shame, is a mirror made of sand & Topeka.
Topeka, you are substandard. I am not. Yet I'm the one on my hands & knees, searching
for the lost keys in the prairie grass, ripped on acid, loving the fallacy that
the black keys equal melancholy, the black keys being Topeka.
Topeka, miscast capital, you're no more political than a handshake with your dream-
self upon waking, in my case dream-self lives & dies in Topeka.
Topeka, the sickness cannot be cured of Topeka.
Topeka, tigers laze about the yards, a man with a box balanced on his head, his
possessions stuffed to brimming, trots down Topeka Ave.
Topeka, the sickness will go unnoticed. The vaccine is composed of rare
sentiments, the kind that love & hate with equal abandon, love & hate,
love & hate, love & hate. Topeka.
Topeka, there was a night when the moon didn't appear but it appeared everywhere else
in the world, what happened that night? Topeka?
Topeka, I fear for your life, the intersection of 29th & California is a portal to Hell. I died
there twenty times in my youth. Today, driving through, I toss a bouquet
of roses to mark my third death, the one that had a soundtrack I can't shake free.
My sister sings it from the shower every morning. Forecast calls for
occasional showers, with the possibility of late-morning sleet, in Topeka.
Topeka, cast off the reliquaries! Call your men to war! Me? I'll be tugging one last hit
from the bong I fashioned out of the shrapnel of Topeka.
Topeka, pop. rarely exceeds one, as in each trip home happens in rewind, stepping back
across the creek, bird in hand throwing up the worm, further back, unbreaking
its wing, bird flying off as if resurrected but from among the living, there I am,
eight years old, seven, six, now a slug of semen sucked back into my father, now,
as the waters roll back across the plains toward the river, a dog coughs up water,
lifts its head, sees nothing, puts its head back down, this, Topeka, is your history,
although it never happened.

INTERNATIONAL RATE

I'm thinking of a number
between one and the end
of this calling card
that burns through the conversation
I've worked out
ahead of time, wherein
I tell you about the glowworms
pocking the garden banks
like uranium-tinted acne scars,
the weaponized stars discharging
our secret narratives, the sudden
bark! of a dog stuck
in its dumb loop chasing fireflies.
I meant to tell you
my face slid off
in the earthquake.
I meant to tell you
anaphora's the disease of the stutterer.
I meant to file a report, upon seeing
the second plane rise
from the mushroom cloud
that was Flight 93, but, too stoned
on the reflection of the rain
on the hood of the car, I penned
an ambiguous note, which started
and ended with the line,
"too painful."
But nothing's too anything.
                                                            Standing in line
at the grocery store, I've spent
these twenty minutes annotating
the smiles everyone's
fitting into, just for the simple pleasure
shopping can afford, and my debit card is
offering nothing. So, what's next?

More of the static
we've assimilated? As if it's natural
to talk like emphysemic robots.
But we do talk. Let me tell you about
the woman I talked to at the office.
She hated her hometown, its nailed-down trees,
its children painted on the fences fencing
in nothing. And that wind she blew out on?
Listen, it blew its vatic kiss at her every day,
even now it puckers
when you walk past
the open window. And I'm dead
to her. What I mean is, I've kept
a picture of her in my wallet.
The windows rattle.
Are you still listening? I heard you cough.
I heard my own cough. It's just the delay.
I can't keep straight.
My passport's
robbing banks.
I don't fingerprint well.
I've been talking for twenty minutes
and I know the connection's
been dead for nineteen.
                                        Moths here
are shaped like death, they appear
like twisted metal
as they spiral the light fixture.

MAY 31, 2005

—on the occasion of Walt Whitman's 186th birthday

It could last forever.
It did not.
It was committed to song
and was sung in times
of great sorrow. Some said
it was an indulgence, the sorrow.
It bled for all of us, including
the human resources manager,
who died in the office fire
that investigators concluded
was arson. It was forgotten,
eventually, though it was resurrected
during the night, years later,
when everyone dreamed the same dream,
and awoke in a fright,
frightened at the thought
that everyone was dreaming the same thing
at the same time. It drove
me to madness. It sang
itself to sleep, sang of itself
to itself. It drove me to madness.
It sang of itself. It sang of a disaster.
It sang of a tsunami.
It sang of a forthcoming plague.
I heard it sung in a bar
by a retired colonel. He, too,
had been driven to madness.
It could not be sung, he sang.
I have tried digital techniques
in an attempt to simulate it.
I have channeled Carlo Broschi.
I have demanded
a recount. He sang these things
because he could not find

adequate means of expressing
it. Driven to madness trying to sing it,
through the single window
the pale force of the afternoon
light on his face revealed
such terrible anguish. The miles
his face has traveled in search of it.
As I was in search
of it. It cannot be even adequately
expressed. It has driven so many
to madness. It has
driven me mad. It could not
last, it did not. It bleeds,
though, for all of us,
bleeds our rust. It weeps
for the dead inside. Its tears
contain the history
of every desert's absent rain.
Its tears contain
the moments of truth.
Its tears are not notes
to its song, but we must
sing them as if they are.
We must skim the muck
from our pools. We must act
in moderation in everything we do.
We must take care not
to mistake its tears for notes
to its song. It has driven me to madness,
the colonel said. My son
was struck by lightning, the colonel
wept as he said this, seven times.
My son is addicted to depleted
uranium, the colonel wept.
My son depleted his inheritance

in search of it. He was driven
to madness. He is on the jukebox,
do you hear it? The pale force
of Carlo Broschi? We must skim
the muck of centuries, no, of millennia
spent wandering deserts in search
of it, the abstraction we've abstracted
into.
It bleeds our rust. This dust. This
afternoon light reveals the motes
of it. The fire was no accident.
We sing of it, the fire. We sing of it,
the sorrow. We sing for the dust
swept into the dustpan, emptied
into the garbage, trucked out
to the dump. A child's bicycle
tossed near. The wheel spins.
An owl does not alight
on it. The owl is not singing it.
Tu-whit. Tu-whoo. Tu-whee.

JONESTOWN

Wrap the dead infants in bags stitched with the precision of Thomas Eakins, such that they are really real. Choose as fabric the vellum sky, interpreted as top-down processing, and the ligature stitched through the bleak weather's spiny column of wind. An oeuvre of dead bodies, or the groans and gasps rushing up the spine, offloading the body's dying wish, which is to be loved like the living are loved. You can have an opportunity, but if the children are left, we're going to have them butchered. This, anomalous? Sheep glisten in the painting's field as they watch the news on a giant television. Sheep to slaughterhouse, from there, into a wallet fashioned from scraps strewn about slaughterhouse floor, bunched with bleating ghosts. Fashion of juntas macerating the local neighborhoods in the wink of a drive-by. Eat the radish, worship the radish. Now go fall in love with the vision of a dog gnawing its tail off.

&

Various addenda aggregating, what with the sky sucked of its chrome, the locket dangling in the din of jangles sprung from the grease trap I'm lately accustomed to calling my lungs. Being so bewildered. With many, many pressures on my brain. Commuter traffic spasms, rain on sick leave, the residents of this state of mind given to nightly patrols, of the carotid and of the whimsy prisms refracting the funhouse light. Seeing all these people behave so treasonous. There was too much for me to put together. What it's coming down to, just a tiny atoll, coughed up by a dozen A-bomb tests, scraping clean the world's lungs, wiping the trough clean, bilious ancestry, a thousand clean dreams of white houses painted over a summer even whiter. The white of this ticked clock's white face. But I know what he was telling me, he was telling me it'll happen. Death of a parish. Listen for it. If the plane gets in the air, even.

&

We can make a strike, raise your arm to stir the daylights, listen to the wind macerate the palms, but we'll be striking against people that we don't want to strike against. A zephyr of light, this time, and a clock composed of ashes, ashes of what? Strike of pompous dimension, taking up valuable space, as the zither is played by the zephyr of light, like this man, this man, laying himself down to listen to the mandolin rehearse the damages, epic as they will be. We'd like the people that caused this, if some people here are prepared, if some people know how to do that, to go into town. But there's no plane. There's no plane. You can't catch a plane in time. This runway stubbled with weeds, all of you shrinking into the barely audible black train of thought. Or, the locomotive uncouples from the first freight car.

&

Massive structure, beloved fawn-like thing, they drop their ladles into the mist. What is that knotted structure, over on the runway, slick with glistening? This morning, they gave us a code that they'd let us know. You can check on that and see if it's on the code. Check in their respiration diaries, as I've listened to each one recite a story that always ends in the collapse of certain totems, always ends in the bliss of automated transport, like a column of wind, just collapsed. Check with Russia to see if they'll take us in immediately, otherwise we die. Check that. Fuck Russia. They started to gasp, at first. I can't exterminate that. Hundreds of birds hovered over, chirping, as birds do, moaning, as they wouldn't stop doing. But to me death is not—death is not a fearful thing. I've never, never, never seen anything like this before. To paraphrase Soupault, I wanted to get rid of absolutely everything, but during the transition from Dadaism to Surrealism, my heart, leaking the fumes of Hell, dialed your cell and emptied the brave circuits and coiled therein, they do possess me. They possess, but the quiet light whispers into the eye. The eye trickles carnage.

&

That we lay down our lives to protest against what's being done.
That we lay down our lives to protest against what's being done.
That we lay down our lives to protest against what's being done.
That we lay down our lives to protest against what's being done.
That we lay down our lives to protest against what's being done.
That we lay down our lives to protest against what's being done.
That we lay down our lives to protest against what's being done.

That we lay down our lives to protest against what's being done.
That we lay down our lives to protest against what's being done.
That we lay down our lives to protest against what's being done.
That we lay down our lives to protest against what's being done.
That we lay down our lives to protest against what's being done.
That we lay down our lives to protest against what's being done.
That we lay down our lives to protest against what's being done.

&

Son, take out the garbage. Don't do it for me. Do it for yourself. Do it for the starving children in Africa. Take your medicine like a man. Bite down hard. [We are born before our time.] [They won't accept us.] Listen to your father when he's talking to you. Don't look at me like that, young man. Speak when you are spoken to. [The criminality of people. The cruelty of people.] Our God is not a benevolent God. When I was your age. Don't talk back to me. [See all those who walked out?] [Mostly white people.] God is watching. No need to tell your mother. Just between you and me. [Because they come after our children,] [and we give them our children,] then our children will suffer forever.

&

Remember, the dead love us in their hearts, which rust with each tear you let fall into the good earth. The radio, that's a different beast, all the tunes slur into the same speech, which starts and ends with the proposition that we are nothing but an infinite list of facts. Here are the facts, then, for the deejay to consider. The congressman has been murdered. (*Music and singing*). The Red Brigade invaded our privacy. They came into our home. They followed us six thousand miles away. The congressman's dead. (*Music only*). The Red Brigade showed them justice. Please get us some medication. It's simple. It's simple. There's no convulsions with it. It's just simple. Just, please, get it. Before it's too late. Get movin', get movin', get movin'.

DEAR CONSOMMÉ

They classed this place up.
Renamed the lounge, same
warped mirrors, same imported
bustle. Hi, consommé, how've
you been? I've got a little
hurt I'd like to share. My jeans
don't fit right. Zipper's broke.
Blue plunge of thought,
discothèque ambition. I'm whisking
mother out of wintergale.
Her claims. Her molt.
She'll do major damage
gleeful & loose-toothed. Brittle
thought that I am, the stars comment
nothing on me. Evaluating
one star-husked night encasing
another, mother-drift sneezed
out the anonymous nose. Open,
tomorrow, earlier than I'd like,
me, policed, locked in, interrupted
without interruption, wind
at my back, spending the next day
locked in the chamber of a bong
sucked into mother's lungs
as she, spent, cast out,
walks off in high dudgeon.

GLYCERIN FOLIO

I worry about you. Mmm. I do.
I moved to a Lifestyle Estate
out of sheer prophecy, settling
on two lambs and a piglet. Why is
it you don't phone in
the ultraviolence, such an outmoded
mode, isn't it, so wild so ad hoc
and ad hominem. I have
heavy artillery, I have lasers,
I have guided imagery.
Last night, watching you walk
through the clearing smoke,
glass pebbling your arm, I was so proud.
Proud to say that I don't know
you anymore, or never did, or never
will. You're welcome out here anytime.
Please leave your backpack
by the shed and listen for the music
coming from the hills
where I'll be watching your approach,
detonator in hand.

THE HUM

The hum phases in. Copy machine. Scanners. Idle. Computers laze in hibernation. Phones receive and dump to voicemail. Your call. "I'm awkwardly filed." Moved over to the boss' corner office. Brought a shank. Consider the light refracting off the buildings. The cleaning lady goes unobserved, but if one appears to be watching her, does she then begin to exist? If one of us steps aside to let her empty the recycling bin, is this empathy? Does she feel the humanity? Let us ask her. "I was wondering if you'd let me tape you while you clean." Does she sleep best after a good night's work? And yet, what passes for thinking today in poetry, one might call it voyeur porn, is carefully staged to appear to have happened casually, such as in this office, after hours, on the boss' desk. "I want to be a better person. I want to be known as 'feeling better.'" Carefully staged to appear to have happened causally, as if one thing always leads to another. The false humility of this poem similar though not the same as the cheer in the receptionist's voice. I give all of me all the time, all the time ticks away in the shape of a digital second hand, which I can reset but cannot manage to stop. Please don't mistake my office persona for the real thing, except I spend the good parts of myself at work, so what is the not-office persona, who is that? He thinks happiness will eventually catch up, but he can't keep his pronouns in order, it's like his tell, and now he is tired. "I'm not wired for this." You must have seen the revolution up close, like in person, we say to the cleaning lady. Her tears are shaped like sickles & hammers. Kidding, kidding. Shaped like stars & bars. Now navigating the clots of traffic as the cleaning lady takes the elevator up, the trash takes another, the floors tick down past zero.

THE SLEEP

touches everyone. The sleep is pinned to the junipers
wracking their collective sunshine for the answer. If only,
one said, we could sleep inside the machine's
breath, we'd dream of the other orchard, the one
that sleeps in cunning, colors in the leafy margins
a cobalt blue sampled from the leaf's imaginings
of sky-as-blue, blue-as-death.
All the sand, too, the cormorant as natural
engine, subject lines, medicated correspondence
bottling its essence in tinctures, tinctures
favoring feverish, feverish describing
the immigrant labor napping beneath us. Too tired
to dream the way the rich dream. Flies collect
on the crust of the sandwich flopping from
one's hand, so restful, the hand, the fly,
the dream inspired by gears turning over,
levers and levels, all the abstraction drawn
into focus. A worker proud of nothing,
the interior homelessness circumscribing
itself around two or three of her best dreams.
An accord with linoleum floor, an accord with
recurring nightmare. An accord with husband
and wife sharing a towel, blesséd towel.

BREAKFAST

Here is your bacon. Listen
to the moths collect when the light
in your head flickers on,

how they sizzle in the pan.
Miniature prototypes
of mechanical flight. The roach

underfoot won't feel a thing.
The view from the window
of the beach leeched

of its tide, spinning tildes
of seagulls, a car door
disarticulated. Outside the trailer,

just another tornado
chucking around town, biding time
in this poem while I scrape through decades

of resin paneling
the inside of my skull.
Today is the tenth anniversary

of your second death,
or the fifth anniversary of your sixth
trip to the room so quiet you could hear

the odd phrase of puke eight doors down,
and you'd recognize it
as another clichéd

response to sobriety,
but a sobering sobriety,
and the nurse so full

of charming
sobriquets for each minute
of this dry run

towards a place you will never recognize,
DT's, shakes, she's even named the pills
after her favorite Disney characters:

Ariel swims through your eyes,
Pocahontas bleaches
your last good memories

of tenure. Time to scramble some eggs.
The moon's double life
as a lamp and a symbol,

and as lamp and symbol.
The sea is a genius of suffering,
as the sky is an epidemic

of small-scale proportions,
though the leaves
rustle with a vulgar mouth's

mouthed vulgarities, such as
a hypodermic slides into
your outstretched arm.

You feel the pain
contract, shunt through the brain
like a piece of cooling lava.

I feel your pain
killers as they communicate
the wetness of pain. Its wet silence.

DAMAGE MANUAL

... banshee light intervals,   morning full
of you unplugging your anxieties,   back in the washroom a shade
showers,
demon breathing in water cooler,   several JPEGs
          a resemblance but that one has
                              brown pubic hair and that one
swallows   and that one
looks directly into the camera so still you continue to look,
                              political overtones to neighborly behavior, still
you must be thinking about that time when your co-worker
                                        touched you,   "under
the table," monstrous mahogany desk littered with, office replacing
Baghdad as most dangerous place on earth, ...

~

                                        ... the little rapes   that go on
                              behind conference room doors, teleconferencing the
new telepathy, you can't write   your way out of a box, when
will it be lunch,   another co-worker
used a copy machine after hours to make an experimental film,
coffee's thoroughly enslaved   your sex drive, making
the switch to a laptop   seemed great
mobility's a good thing, right   until that trip, another co-
worker offered to watch   your iPod
while you went to lunch, ...

~

... lunch alone taking the F train
               to the library, some fake explosion holds things up,
have to get on downtown train just after stepping off, ...

~

... a co-worker's boyfriend left her,   "I'm not
crazy,"
cubicle over making speech about mental states, control over them,
she won't be coming back,
sometimes the water cooler makes love,
still looking for picture,
you are salaried so no breaks,
they've been sitting behind those doors all day breaking only for
group sex behind closed doors,
office rumor,
nobody really has sex they just spread seed in chat rooms,
coming out of the washroom once they said,
other times you don't come out, ...

~

... "we fucked in my office last night,"
shipments arrive at the warehouse,
firewall makes intimacy impossible,
at one point everyone in reverse,
smiling at the wall,
cube mate sick all week,
herpes going around the office be careful in the washroom, they're
still in conference making decisions,
what do you think they think of you,
if they think of you,
day winds down no surplus to keep desk chair under you, ...

~

... trying to meditate on the cursor   mantra blinks eye
blinks dignity blinks, you've become super aloof, there's a pubic
hair stuck   in the keyboard
under the "P" key,   word around the office
                                this morning, keep losing focus, what

prison am I in, maudlin receptors light up, sky is the enemy,
window the pain, review this afternoon, measuring time
in letters typed this makes 386, the
second person I spoke with today wasn't you, water
cooler experiment went awry, data-munging fills me up,
what can the office environment yield,
co-workers don't just sit and
stare at screen they shift in their seats and
interior is like Donkey Kong, ...

~

... heel broke at deli, lunch alone in cyclone I am
dessert for scaffolding, walked like a tourist nervous
detailing experience with chamois, they say "New York minute"
which is lifespan of ennui which is, DIY salad already
lost its luster, ...

~

... twenty minutes then review,
washroom habit attended to,
Brando just died,
everyone in the office has an opinion,
manager conducts review in mock-bravado
"You either nut up or you don't,"
pushed things as far as he could,
for instance asking if my "bush resembles Ben Wallace or Chauncey Billups,"
I don't play basketball,
I consider filing a report but to whom,
three percent raise,
enough to justify upgrading Nerve.com account,
still looking for sky wide as tide at Fire Island beach where O died, ...

~

... blight on the company's antiquities, shelf of understanding
collapsed over the weekend, memos
retiring another handful of shale, temp asks for
directions to washroom, weekend pulses a throbbing
gloss over morning emails, need filter
or vacuum, cube mate's
disappeared again left behind office diary, eat page upon page
to clear my stopped up system, since
the you's have been left off for today, being asked
to create a presence at the desk behind
me to mask the lack thereof,
investors on their way over, I keep doing
the math, the math swirls in my head
coffee cooled while I spun through my addition can I bill for this
behavior, ...

~

... boss won't let us leave early to vote,
so I've "paired up" with a Naderite in Ohio,
manager of my section teabagged last night after "wild night"
celebrating his raise,
pictures going around,
just asked to attend conference in Toledo,
saw body parts of motorcyclist strewn across highway fresh upon scene of
accident on road just outside Toledo,
on the way home you might forget to pick up milk,
distracted, as you are, by the video art you once called "life,"
now he loosens his tie when he leans against the cube wall, ...

PALM TREES / 1

Referring to microscopic things, which I cannot see and therefore cannot describe. Ganglia, Angola, Golan Heights, chromosomes, someone's at the door. Referring to the window through which I observe our neighbors. They have collected their deck furniture and put it inside for the last time before they leave for Mexico. Rather be anywhere than here, sitting at my desk, converting files. Everything here is an establishing shot, and once something has been established, what happens next?

PALM TREES / 2

LAX, for example, then Sepulveda Boulevard. Papering palm tree cutouts over holes in the sky. Riding shotgun in my friend's shitty Celica, having driven past the Death Star, local parlance for the new CAA building. A building designed to convey contempt. Palm trees wink past. We're not even moving and they appear as one long blur, prompting me to signal to my friend to pull over. Emotion sickness, linked to nostos, which as an idea doesn't travel all that well, buried as it is in the various nostalgias tricked out on billboards every fifty feet. "Take a Risk," one says. A lesson in aesthetics, the sky is, painterly in its way, bad art. But the palms, how they terrify me. Beginning to think the world radiates from this car. And that man asleep on the bench, warming the sidewalk with a pool of urine, beard crushed into the neck of his Army jacket, his cracked toes sticking out of the cardboard he has carefully crafted into boots, this man so looks the part I am certain he is only openly auditioning. One never knows when somebody who matters might get stuck in traffic right here, as we are, somebody who needs a few authentic extras for background dressing on some movie set. It's easy to say the homeless aren't a problem in this town. They aren't. They have yet to be discovered.

PALM TREES / 3

There is an empty chair in a painting by Richard Diebenkorn that hangs in the Nelson Atkins Museum in Kansas City, on which I used to sit from time to time. Nobody could see me but I would sit there and smoke, rub the ashes into the floor with my heel. I don't remember what this looks like. The last thing I remember before I left Kansas was how easy it was to forget I was there, jogging on a stone road surrounded by wheat. Upon reaching the end of the road I would take a moment to catch my breath and take everything in, the empty sky, the traffic on I-70, the seizure of bees pollinating the wildflowers. The last thing I remember before leaving Kansas was how easy I knew it would be to forget these things, and that all I really wanted was to not die there.

PALM TREES / 4

The war is happy to be alive. Today's report calls for drear as far as the mind can see. In debt to the shadow creeping over my lung, I will compose a letter to my creditors wherein I will confess to everything. But for now, more ramen. For now, I'll pretend you think I'm still going to enlist. I want to shoot the enemy. I want to protect your right to peel potatoes in the buff. I want to be happy to be alive.

PALM TREES / 5

My last defense is the present tense. The polis polish the dew
on the grassy knoll as the lone gunmen sync their watches.

PALM TREES / 6

The methadone clinic flowers into paradise. Bring out the confetti. I mean it. Shit's getting screwy. I don't function like the others. I'm part mafia, part ghost net, shades of Dubai. I walk down Clark in Cinemascope and I end up at a cemetery. It's like I'm twelve again, introducing my hand to the rest of my body. I didn't figure 34'd be the new twelve. It doesn't compute. What is the it? My wife breaking her hand breaking her fall? There's all kinds of things one can take for this. The thingness between her thighs. Mutual appreciation. We can afford to knock over the Brinks truck parked in front of our local Starbucks because we've concluded that it's better to feel alive than to be alive. Skinny latte!

PALM TREES / 7

At MOMA. Certain intellects instruct me that I'll fall in love with figuration all over again once I see the show. I see nothing but blobs. America is not eating enough. Or too much, depending on New York. All my friends are frying eggs in Park Slope condos. Every time you open your mouth, I want to vivisect a deer. This is known as synaesthesia. You say, "I don't understand you anymore," and all I see is confetti misting the room.

PALM TREES / 8

Under *this* volcano. Green light flashes from above the tree line. Two ex-pats experience the native land by introducing this country town to Rohypnol. A small terrorist act, letting fall a few drops into hers and hers drinks. I am reading a late draft of my father's primer on psychosexual development. This version reads like a memoir. Now two German backpackers go missing and, obsessed with Scientology, the Berlin papers somehow miss it. They just disappear. Nobody has ever come back. For all we know, it's like Eden. The undisturbed among us decamp and make a run for it. My sweet globalism, how can I repay you for my broadband connection this deep in the jungle, this close to the sun! Doctors cut out a mass from my mother's hairline, leaving five stitches behind. A precaution. How I miss my mother, in the most lucid way, the way she always wanted to be missed. Only today, observing the native flora — listening to the palms grow (it sounds like fucking) — do I recognize my error. When she told me she wanted to be anonymous, it wasn't a joke, though it had nothing to do with staying free from some megalithic database. It is like this fern in my sights, it would prefer me to look the other way.

PALM TREES / 9

The vapor, the needle, the one person who won't stop reading what I write. I actually believe I can erase my parents' imprint on me by thinking of such a thing happening. Waiting... still waiting... happened. Whole new world. Got a call from someone claiming to have my best interests in mind. He knew my SSN, which I did not. He now has complete control over my stock portfolio. Who would've figured me for having a portfolio? Wow. I am really liking this. I just met my sisters in Barcelona and minutes later I ditched them for Ibiza. I don't have sisters, not like that. And these blondes, they just accumulate like newspapers at my door. Where are they coming from? I am now the subject of a documentary an "old friend" is making about my amnesia. I clock time on beaches, experiencing the tide like it's my first lay. Oh my God, the tide!

PALM TREES / 10

Even turning the sheets down, the skeptical alliance of thirsts, man overboard, crack rock making a comeback, so we kept things to ourselves, mostly. All this fuzzy interior, gondola of the mind, from this distance, the mountains appear to be covered in grass. Last night my addiction to you resurfaced so I detoxed on the U.S. Open. Federer the Feline vs. the Russian Fixer. Gorgeous backhand down the line. Off kilter he slaps his racket at the Impossible, returns it down the line for break point. The kind of devastation Federer visits upon Davydenko is not unlike the time I have spent editing your manuscript, watching one improbable image after another, the breaking of syllables, the lines scrolling through the interior like sea snakes in the nightmare my brother is locked into and stares out of.

PALM TREES / 11

This streaming life. Our contiguousness, our resilience, our shapeliness. Our vogue. What, after all, is a starling today? Or the Baltics? Globalist tankers lined up in English Bay, the yellow mounds of sulfur viewed from the shore as we run the seawall in Stanley Park, a sun perpetually setting, remind me of my addiction to dusk, an addiction to the twilights of addiction. Memory only reminds me that I continue to forget things. Friends come and go to Mexico. Family sits on the porch of Wichita wondering who rewound the sea.

PALM TREES / 12

I did the kudzu poem. The one about God. About Paris. My mother's tremors. When my sister shot the Pope I was there, writing a poem. My first drive-in movie. Back seat stuff, really wild. Makes you blush. I am a light box, a cascade of light! So I wrote all these poems. I cashed checks, stared at tellers as they stared into specific oblivions. Came up wanting. Where is there more? In the box you come from the box under the bed. No more starlings no more pregnant loaves of bread. No more no more. Yes, I incandesce. Starlings spill out from the windows. Refreshing beer in hand makes me happier than. All the leaves are. This is Wellington, friend, drive she said just keep your wheel in the religion you'll spin a bit and then it goes crunch! They all grind their children into a fine, millennial dust.

PALM TREES / 13

My anger is a clock pulling yesterday into it. When I read about amputee children in Darfur, I quietly click through to the iPhone demo. My anger is dick-shaped and in search of the hole at the end of the universe. Back when I was a farm is when I loved you in the shade, the curve of your back, the glass lung I blew for you, how it caught the late afternoon light in such a way as to just dazzle us, snatch our breath.

PALM TREES / 14

Neither on TV nor on Japanese fan nor replay of nightmare sharks vomit seals, buildings that have fallen resurrect, politely, someone asks for a serviette, a doily, anything that sounds baroque. The lost data ebbing at the bottom of the neighbors' pool really was their son's body, decomposed into numbers.

PALM TREES / 15

I woke up to the sound of the TV chewing through the ceiling, woke up to my heartbeat gnawing its ration of speed, woke up at the bottom of Lake Michigan clutching my manuscript, woke up wingless, scattered to the asps, woke up the neighbors with double-pump action putting their dog down, woke up in a clausal phrase you'd edit out, & handing you a red pen you redlined my married sister — "just dropped by for a quick 'hello' after work" — I should've knocked — putting a roll of our toilet paper in her purse.

PALM TREES / 16

In this world, the unrated world, we get to do whatever we want. The unicorn spearing the city in its gut. The fashion of home movies, boy sets out for bigger & brighter, eyes gleaming a life living in the hazardous fray of jump-cuts. Pool's edge. A salt lick of coke. The zoo, where Silverback apes grieve the dead. One sniffs the stiff body, laid in wake. Its nose strolls every inch, as if down a boulevard clearcut through the jungle, searching for something recognizable. Another surveys the body, rests its head on an outstretched arm. The zookeeper told reporters she cried herself into a headache. People are eating each other in the North. But in the South, comrade, a little girl stokes a campfire as the shadows multiply, as a stick breaks underfoot, and underfoot is the first break of dawn.

PALM TREES / 17

Take my hand — do you know such ecstasy, its blowback, kissing you, mistakenly, all analgesic evening, eating mushrooms a hue, a spritz, you can't conflate the shapes, unmerciful enterprise, we're awaiting our face, code look we split, two voices/either ear, a conscience, a guilt, a tavern drunk through, tiny light lights your, what? How Balthus of you, Commodore, spanking your vatic self silly, but you dare to repeat, we understand your conversion's an I you won't dot, the lemming you are, people are staring, wobble on, cane and all, perfect the slurry sermon, Sunday's got a bead on you.

PALM TREES / 18

Now we're f*c#ed, soundtrack trimmed from the budget, and must go with the image alone. Search engine trauma, lilac inversion tells truth light switch style. Standing on a box of munitions taped to brainwet, acrostic speech pattern: for u can't know evil's depths. Will each thought demand self-sale or linger in the dank dark, linger to rot? Whitecapped cubicle mountain conquered as the enemy pins flag to lapel pins finger to temple. Wonder why tattered sky? The cloudbank slits its wrists last huff and puff of the wolf spills out. People still care enough to send their very best young men to build prisons in the desert where a century of penal research frays one prisoner at a time into an echo. Why persist, you ask? Why not. Always this feeling better feeling. Bored in Iraq one Government Issue reads another cover to cover, free to form his/her own opinion. Easily converts to Jeep with rack & pinion steering, roams Baghdad like skip-trace. Woman slips between buildings holding a bundle. Everywhere you look an afterlife heckles.

PALM TREES / 19

He frolics in the taxis' orgiastic swell. He rays. He summons. He clicks. After a while, he uploads everything. Cameron was a friend of his. As was Sofia. They smoked the Paris blunt. Everything fell away, turned corpse blue. Bowler on the green lawn, die for him. Violent sea of awe, remain in awe. He pilots the narcotic classrooms squared into airplanes. He screams. He complies. Such majesty, such grace. He unhinges all the doors. Beverly vivisects Chauncey. The ash heap rolled into the Dubai blunt. Streetlamps froth. He concurs, after all this downtime whistling after the dogs. He whites the blacks. He browns the yellows. Acid rain beads on his bed-soft tongue. The girl paddling a surfboard to intervene in the whale's demise is harpooned. He rolls her into the Atlantic blunt, passes her around Cape Cod, comforting his lungs with an intravenous drip of pure snow. He has his sublime imported from China's vagina. He crashes. Cameron the figment. Sofia the Coppola. Paris was a joke, a riot. He grids down. Whitecaps flatten. Polar caps, what, they melt? That was yesterday. Today, he joins the mutants to pluck the sinewy remains. He prepares to discover fire. The lassitude and longitude of the Topeka blunt. Numbers flash everywhere. Chauncey flash-freezes Beverley. He goes viral. He hacks the yellow blood. He opens a book, declares it a tree. Boarding the El, he forgets he cannot stare like this, they will think he's on to something. He baptizes every one of them on the third rail. This close to the sun, this fucking close.

PALM TREES / 20

Fever breaks into dream. The man cycling ahead of me as I jog through Andersonville, is it my friend who left for Colorado, or was it Mexico? I can't catch up, he turns the corner. No matter. It is not him, I am sure of this. I am thinking now of the cold to come, the swells, the decline in crime that attends the end of summer. Less looking over my shoulder, less concern for my wife on her commute. Maybe we will spend a weekend climbing sand dunes. I wrote, "Grease taking shape of one lung, then the other," two years ago, and I no longer recognize myself. This used to be the aim. I once wrote, "My belief is insubstantial. My clamp, my valve, my love / of the folded number."

PALM TREES / 21

When I stepped onto the sidewalk today I heard a car backfire not as a gun. I heard it simply as a car backfiring. I was liberated. The children on the corner unhinged their jaws. They wanted to swallow me, but Ben reassured me that I'd make it home, and that you'd still be there. He didn't actually say anything, it was more how he didn't react. A world in a gesture, that kind of thing. When we got to the park, I suggested we walk backwards, retrace our path exactly. I had missed something, though unsure of myself, and asked Ben if he felt the same. I never feel the same, he said. The sidewalk unspools under each heavy step. Twemlow, he added, your sickness is your lack of sickness; this puzzles me. Loss blossoms, my love, nocturne disappoints, the wind swivels the window lock open. I am climbing further back into the wave, disconsolate, hardly there. I am sleeping less than four hours a night. I am sleeping like an addict in search of an addiction. Night sweats out night upon night of the morepork's morose call. What, lonely bird, do you lament? What blossoms in your migrations from one moment to the next? I see the faces of all the good people pinch into question marks as they watch the sky crack open. After I'm gone, who will stop to consider this awkward butterfly, slurring from tree branch to porch rail, that hawks the latent, indivisible dream, adrift in the history of air, its spastic circulars of flight, death nearing, as is its wont, and with that final swish of its wings, exactly nothing happens?

MOUTH BREATHER

This town drips
its sewage right into
your mouth. Tea cools
on the table, frogs
miasmic with the wind.
I am in awe of the poet
in awe / giddy
at the world /
famously in love with every-
thing! Syllabic
love, meretricious love,
illicit, disturbed, mendacious
love! O to be one
with the tenacious
among us. Awe replaces
guilt, guilt
replicates pumping gas
at the Kum & Go while
one's cat boils in the heat
in the backseat. Bed
down in this community
of rucksacks and antediluvian
daydreams, the porch
in need of a good sweep,
the books remain un-
published, the gods
fuck every open hole.
Call me Animal, call me
anytime you're
sizing up the chandelier
for a noose. Your bourbon's
warmed to a nosebleed.
The bank teller hydraulics
your life's work, returns
slips of paper dot-matrixed

with your symbolic life
teeming like bedsores
you later turn over to
scribble a few words
the radio voice whispered
into commercial:
black helicopters over
America, more after
the break. Motel parking lot
ripples in the heat;
it's the tar baking,
and in Room 26 your
future spreads its legs
on the edge of the mattress,
fidelity just a word
I flipped past on the way
to fuck me. Dust spits up
and screams its name,
a child's name, the diabolic
intensity revealed
dusting the art on the walls
of our new home.
                    Nobody to read
                                        these
missives. I write as if
there's audience
in arrears, flowing
from the back channels
beyond media,
tapping a spring
called The Source. Pe-
trarch sold his proclivity
for the prehensile
in this spot. Tourists
sip their espressos,

I wand forth a waiter
with a paltry croque-
monsieur, my wife
crabs a glass of hot water,
all the world sifting
through me, this
error in the
transcript long since
yellowed into fact.

A HUMID HOLE, WHICH IS BREATHING

The pain started here. It resembled
Nothing I had. My arm tethered
To a balloon. A humid hole,
Which is breathing, which said
God is dead. Halitosis. God is me
On acid, whittling my thumb
Into a coin, which I may forever
Insert into vending machines.
This is righteous, spoke the native.
Bespoke native, pelt sac, Tā moko,
Centuries of unmediated anger
Unleashed on the body. Register
Rings up tonal shifts, expensive ones.
Mother loved me most flaccid.
Gangrene nightmare, the folly
Of nudism. Every hole opens
To sing a song about the starlings
Diving into the hole opening
Between your eyes. God is thanked
For making this dunk possible.
For me, God drinks milk,
Milks all the possibilities
On the table. A corporate God,
Bespoke suit, vellum skin,
Precisely enunciated vowels.
End-stopped bowels.
Every slick sentence milked
& bilked, sliced & diced.
Every humid hole
Breathes in at once, an example
Of mass hypnosis. I don't mean
To be so arch. I just don't know
How to be otherwise. The hive,
The hole, the corruption. I press
A pimple on my nose. Liquefied

Sunrise washes the strychnine
From my system. Hollandaise?
Absolutely. I have my father's
Heart, a love of orphaned creatures
Aflame in alleyways, and his ability
To rage indifferent to alliances.
What I mean is, I will destroy
Your hyoid bone the moment
You light the match you throw
Onto the dog you've soaked
In kerosene, consequences be damned.
That's a politics, an ethos, a dirge.
We love rain-soaked puppies.

PASTEL

Remain saturated to the point of hegemony,
all these trees tinged with dropsy dystopia,
heart on my sleeve bridging its last beat
with second stanza of lost Goldberg

variation, variation on a theme that screams
theocracy's lungs out from the bottom rung
of civility, wherein machete lops in a stutter
of dropped frames, gnats flood the eye,

& if I hesitate to record. As I said to my cube mate,
"I've been to your church. Your church sucks.
But we do all this
for the same Guy, right?"

"Dog fell apart laughing at lugubrious louse
weeping whilst working the crease from
my pants. Never meta-woman I didn't
paint her portrait in splattertones."

I'd been given to writing such lines   such lines!
some months ago when I had given up
hope the dog down the street'd
end up bankrupt, sire of three pups by three

bitches, fuzzy dice dangling over each newborn's
crib. That kind of life I smoke through
when I'm out of weed, wherein
the Brads accumulating like snowdrifts

in my reruns of high school
end up like that.
misremembered
where my tent is   naked wandering thru

forest of dune buggies
people think he's
him like
stereo-care when

peril washed in w/tide
theirs the way they hide fleece
mantle Argonaut
but when sometimes

the sun shits in my ear
pang & desist,
& I overheard my dealer on his cell whisper
directions to my apartment, down to the extra

jiggle the doorknob requires, next thing
I'm knocking on an apartment door
I don't recognize, waiting for an answer.
Which is code for I'm sort of an indentured

servant, but that's the boring, obsessional side
of addiction, who isn't afraid their partner's
brokering deals with Syria or Iran?
My wife's the exception, but even she

turns blue when all the words match up,
& she's lately been carrying nukes in her nook,
the implication being that a turntable is still able
to reverse antiquity. You've seen it in boardrooms

mahogany sheen to the brow of the man
putting for the company title.
"Data? I didn't even know her,"
then some remix of the conversation over a wet lunch.

As the sun sets on the American Century,
the abstract clavicle also tenderly put to cheek
in one of many "human moments"
the last surviving member of the Donner

Party wiped constantly from the brow
of nostalgia. But when I was a little boy, around five, I saw
my mother inside the jaws of a great white shark
& terrifically dressed, she lit a flame in its belly

but the Dead Sea, god, is a mistake, reverse engineering
for the progress in us, minions, minnows, the sea
the salt, I've grown tired of not being able to exhibit
my sadness to others, the mug shots, orange

jumpsuits, the sinners hogging floor space.
One held my ankles, another pinned my wrists
to a hot plate, the third put his mouth around
my ear and told me he had "too many new ideas

& stories crowding" his head, he was crazy
for wanting to put his dick in my mouth.
I told him I had an agent unafraid of
representing Delphic Oracles, so he recites

a story of a cloned white tiger with an almost
human brain (what's the missing ingredient?)
take control of the life of his owner
in a horrifying way by spreading blood
from its eyes. He pled for me to give him a chance.
He also writes action stuff. I told him I'd
bite. He called my bluff.
I need to bleed the river of truth. Fascicle

for the sad inside, street team smearing
me over the drear of last night's whiteout.
I know what I should do. I should
take off my shoe. Serenity
now, the promise crystal
meth makes with an armbar.

But I love the drugs I can get in this town.
Said meth flowering like flowers,

roadside fruit stands wink in the periphery
as I near the wall at such great speed, Las Vegas,
it could've been Phoenix, such insane slay
of daylight. MRI bores a sonic hole in my head,

tumor's twitched into a lake view estate fronted
by a swinging gate. A trembling leaf falls
from an apple tree, rich with shame. & someone
please remind my wife to read this when I die.

"Honey, please forgive the histrionics, but I somehow
got stapled into the wrong journal. Please
print the errata & slip it into the memorial program.
Otherwise, I'm your *casus belli* (I hacked

the Pentagon mainframe & typed 'in bed' at the end
of each line of code (that's just the tumor
doing its best Shari Lewis; you'd be surprised
how lonely, and thus ornery, it gets)) in case

your despair goes on hiatus & you start
preparing for each student conference
like it's war." Let me be clear.
I am occasional. I deliver on a promise,

so if I say I will drive a stake through your heart,
fit your coffin. You are useless, dead.
This is the true Twemlow.
Whether you know my name or not,

be assured I am feeling it,
feeling Twemlow, that eternal, brandied optimism.

Trust me, when I tell you his name.
His sidekick will crush your knee.

THE PINES

Memory of coi
Splashes
This afternoon
A wash of gray, a garish gray
Swells

That boy will cut
His finger
On not just the edge
Of this afternoon
But forever thinking
Tied into a cot,
Now

The lonely gray elephant
With its otherworldly
                                        Horns

I HATE KARATE

I see you seeing me. I wonder wonder wonder what will become of you. I hate that I hate, but alas, I still hate. I seethe. Karate can go fuck itself. Can kill itself. Can fight itself to the death. That's what karate does. It's all about ratings. I hate ratings. I hate ratings so much I develop my own reality show. In this show, you, viewer, are asked to watch me hate. I'll hate anything. But I'll hate karate first and foremost. I hate karate when I'm strung out and panhandling on the corner where I grew up and happy to accept a farthing. I hate karate when my credit card is declined and I've got formula and diapers and wipes and a baby that hasn't stopped crying since I was born. I am a master of the hate. I'll hate anything you present to me. Robert Creeley? Hate him. My cancer-stricken mother. Hate her. Your photos of your child and the delicate balance you maintain between love and work. Dress me up in a suit made of hate, stitched together by ten-year-old Indonesian children. Then, watch me hate them, their piety, and their sleepless nights, their fingers worked to the bone. I hate Steve Jobs. He hate me? Then there's enough hate in this world to keep it spinning. Like a dreidel made of razor blades. I'll give one to my son on the first day of Hanukkah, and tell him that when he sees blood, it's just the color of all those who have hated you since you first walked the earth. You, destined to wander and negotiate, grovel, plead and every other mode of humiliation that can be imagined. Because, my son, you have been hated on since your God asked Abraham to make the ultimate sacrifice. This Christmas season, when I sit you on Santa's fat and happy lap, give him this dreidel. Better: shove it in his mouth and tell him to bite down hard. When he bleeds his hate, tell him you were sent to purify his soul, his pitiless, black soul filled with lumps of coal, themselves the very essence of hate. Don't hate the hater, my son. The hand that spins the dreidel comes from above. It is the hand of hate. It is your salvation.

FOREIGN AFFAIRS

So this is Eighteen Hands of the Lo Han.
Spear hand to the sternum. Cross shuto
to the ribs. You want to locate
the precise moment when a reverse punch
to the face might
enfeeble an army
of shit-serious anarchists
hell-bent on keeping the withering
sanctions intact. Back knuckle
to the groin'll show 'em.
Ridge hand to the temple. A necklace
of ears & a hammer fist
goddamn square on the bridge
of the nose. Solder the x/y
to the otherwise sexless
killing machines. Double fist
to the ribs & groin.
Repeat these secret strikes
like you've got privilege coursing
through your veins. Back knuckle to the face.
Bend & flex
the arm with all the grace you place
the dessert fork above the dinner plate.
Double shuto to the neck and ribs.
Ridge hand to the groin.
Six-year-old kid smiles
senile when uppercut
to the jaw
blows his fecal little village
to pieces. He's got the shakes
& being taught
spear hand to the bladder
he understands
how a flower morphs
into a daisy cutter & how thin

the line between.
Straight up shuto to the face.
It's basics. Like diplomacy.
Like a palm heel to the heart.
Buckle up little shell-shocked
son of some gladly erased.

CLOSEWORK

My anger controls the orange groves burning at the horizon.
The horizon, my endless question.
I was breaking down in tears emailing shelters to try and find someone to take her in today.
Please don't act like I'm stupid and waste time on stock replies.
I've heard it all
hinges on how stable your hands remain upon insertion.
Always talk as if the person you are speaking to is wearing a wire.

WITH DELICATE HAND

Never instead put the bales in the bounty,
resize the type to provide ALLURE.
Look how the picture seems to tell a story.

Mother, I'm all dolled up in HOPE.
My breastplate hinge needs a little oil,
I'm hobbling along to kick your crutch.

Mother, I'm all doped up with DESIRE.
I've cleaned the machine with delicate
hand, scrubbed the data within an inch of its life.

Mother, I'm all diary today, feeling PENSIVE.
The returns keep disappearing, I can't get my hands
around even one. I keep clicking through

the channels, the links, little vortex
displays all the characteristics of a MOTIVE,
Mother, but someone's just reported

that the election has been made OFFICIAL.
The results seem promising. In one version
you get to keep the crown. The twin diamonds

sparkling your eyes sparkle harder, the LIGHT
takes on a decadence like that of old snow.
In the other, your garland consumes itself,

your hair falls out like nuclear, your elisions
lisp the windows shut, breaking the view
in half. Your face becomes but a VAGARY

and there are no backups in storage. I AM
a cosmos if I am still breathing. Wind breaks
at my neck and spells your name acrostically.

spells your name like my BELOVED. Repetition
of facts and figures keeps me apprised. Dogs
mass in the streets, shaking bones, slurping scrap

lifted from the MALFEASANCE of silver plates
hung to dry from row house clotheslines,
the tread's worn down on the spires sagging

from the GLORIOUS peaks of this great sky!
Can you hear the clicking through the air vents?
Did you notice the picture twitch on the bedroom wall?

Leaves turn pink and blue, SUPERNATURAL
is not dead, is rippling through me, I can feel
my toes, I can see you staring at my nape,

I can see you vivid in the dark corner of the day,
taking your damask gown off one strap
at a time, as if I were watching. I have a MANDATE.

Nobody else would bother to see you this way.

AGONY & X

—for ALC

I have no right to engage this so I engage this. The chakras fly apart. My whole inner self turns from the mirror reveals agony. I am so just kidding. I'm naked in the bathtub soaking in Old Milwaukee. I am listening to planets collide. I am in bed with her. It is quiet. You are still alive somewhere out there. I am now begging her to kiss me. I am weeping. I am listening to planets collide. I am jacked into the moment. She relents. Her lips are possibly quivering but she kisses me. You are a freeze frame. I am frying in a bathtub of toasters. I am picturing you getting out of the car and running after the bus vaguely aware of me laughing. I am listening and I hear you wheezing. I am staring at clown drawings tacked up on your wall. You are never going to wake up from something unlike a dream unlike a vision. Planets collide. I am visiting you in order to absolve myself of my vague past. I break down on occasion when I think about what happened. The past is a wire hanger and a back alley and a problem. I am beginning to think everything happens in hotel rooms. I am in the downtown Holiday Inn and she is asleep and someone is at the door. You are barely able to move and sometimes you must feel like this is how it is. I am certain I have never known a silence as tender as that hotel room on this night. The person at the door was more than I could bear and he wouldn't say who it was or what happened. That person is knocking at every door you close behind you. The next place you go is heavenly or is shaped like a mouth. You are an archive of documents being scanned by you. I am certain that the sound of planets colliding isn't supposed to be this quiet. Let's just say it. You died that night and no one would tell you. This descent into the sentimental is what might save you. I am writing this to save you. My mistake was to ask you to read this. If we can dispense with psychological interpretations we will sleep better. I am happy you died. I am glad to have known you then but am much happier to know you now. You are reading this after a day of scanning old documents and as you drift into sleep, imagine waking up tomorrow for the first time then wake up tomorrow for the first time. Take notes in a notebook describe the light the people the expression on anyone's face. Leave the notebook somewhere you will find it and not recognize it and scan it and email it to me. Your first entry will describe the grove of lemon trees where you are sitting writing to me about the first woman you were able to talk to about something that happened a long time ago. I'll leave this poem for you to transcribe.

MY LIFE WAS NOVALIS

Flapped in the interminable winds,
see-sawed in the loop
of playground. Novalis.
Say it with me. Novalis.
Rhymes with a specific kind of
internal bleeding, when the ulcer
intensifies, I pour my guts out.
Please video this. Star me
in your parable. My life was Novalis.
Battered round the cape by winds
interminable, Mont Blanc
a mere elegy, and yet when I type
my life begins inside the astronaut
sleeping inside my deepest secret.
The lost pilot spins out of orbit,
collapses the difference between
a head cold and ahead, the cold
stretches out forever, or almost,
for at its end, Novalis.

THE JOY OF SOLIPSISM

Bring the oncoming train into focus.
Tell me your theory of the market.
Pupils dilate, trees fall,
I practice transference in my downtime.
Think of my mother watering
plants. Is
everybody really watching?
Blog me. Add to my Wiki entry.
Date me. Reply to my electronic flirt.
My mother told me she'd nominate
me for that award, if she could bear
the proxy. Show me your tits.
I shaved my balls. I took out
a second mortgage. Motherhood
frightens the elms, carves its sorry
initials into the sky's prolapsed anus.
Each sadness passes through
me like a gallstone. My valve leaks
an amniotic canopy over the
bar I'm fragging. I'm a fragment,
a tender button. I saw my first
beetle in the periphery. Lake Shore
Drive against the ruins, the stain
of lake-effect snow a special effect,
the only weather
exhibiting any real affect.

TRAFFIC CRASH REPORT

You will learn the same techniques.
I'm sorry about the redistricting
of your left hemisphere. The comeback
of the amygdala has been staved
off by the arrival of a stray cat.
Where else would you expect
to find me in a shambles, but the
corner where two station wagons
meet in a perpetual collision?
I'm blanking on your name.
You don't need to train constantly.
The attack will come as a surprise
at your office, the pink slip
a coupon for three nights at a reduced rate
of speed, a recipe for lasagna the CEO's
wife cobbled together, a bullet engraved
with your initials. Though further
inspection reveals your co-worker's
former mailing address tattooed
around your ankle. That was a terrific
bender, last night. I never saw
our son in just that way. There are twenty-four
intense lessons wherein you will
learn the skills needed to recognize
yourself in your wife's compact mirror,
de-escalate potential energies, subdue
a tennis racket, and eliminate a life-
threatening attacker. There simply
is not enough time in an hour, lest you
think I'm joking try packing all your things
in your cubicle into a brown corrugated box.
You have learned the same
techniques, but you seem to have mastered
them much faster than I expected. I have no answer
for why the light coming from the other room

seems so brittle, like when I touch it
and there is nothing in me that believes
in the correlation between it shattering
and my faltering interest in your stories
about the sky falling, splitting open,
or the gate swings shut. The Aeolian harp
blasts a tune sour with rotten fruit. I
want to break the jeweler's window
and place my eyes on display.

THE GREEN LANTERN PRESS

Founded in 2005, The Green Lantern Press is an artist-run, non-profit press focused on emerging or forgotten texts in order to bridge contemporary experience with historical form. We celebrate the integration of artistic mediums. We celebrate the amateur, the idealist and those who recognize the importance of small independent practice. In a cultural climate where the humanities must often defend themselves, we provide intimate examples of creative thought.

Dedicated to the "slow media" approach, The Green Lantern Press conceives each book as a curatorial site; small editions are printed with artist plates, ephemeral inserts, and silk screen covers. We are efficient about the material we use, economic about our proportion and intent on local production.

To step beyond the bounds of a single book, the press is partnered with The Paper Cave—a for-profit bookstore—and The New Corpse—a salon-style performance space—in order to support artists, writers, discourse and community. These relationships form alternative and sustainable models for the presentation and distribution of contemporary art.

OTHER BOOKS FROM THE GREEN LANTERN PRESS

ARTS ADMINISTRATOR'S SKETCHBOOK edited by Elizabeth Chodos & Kerry Schneider, printed in edition of 500, hand bound w/ silkscreen covers by Mat Daly, 2007. Printed in an edition of 700, 2007. $20

THE BRIGHTEST THING IN THE WORLD: THREE ESSAYS FROM THE INSTITUTE OF FAILURE by Matthew Goulish, introduction by Jane Blocker, w/ color plate supplied by author and silkscreen covers by Sonnenzimmer. Printed in edition of 500, 2012. $20

CLOPS by Devin King, introduction by Peter O'Leary, w/ color plates by artist Brian McNearney. Printed in edition of 250, 2010. $10

THE CONCRETE OF TIGHT PLACES by Justin Andrews, introduction by Stephen Rodefer, w/ postcard insert supplied by author and silkscreen covers by Sonnenzimmer. Printed in edition of 500, 2009. $20

FASCIA by Ashley Donielle Murray, w/ silkscreen covers by Sonnenzimmer. Printed in edition of 500, 2009. $20

FORGERY by Amira Hanafi, introduction by Stephen Lapthisophon, w/ color plates supplied by author and silkscreen covers by Dan MacAdam of Crosshair. Printed in edition of 500, 2010. $20

FRAGMENTS by David Carl, introduction by Joseph Fuller, w/ color plates by Mathias Kristersson, and silkscreen covers by Alana Bailey. Printed in an edition of 500, 2008 $20

GOD BLESS THE SQUIRREL CAGE by Nick Sarno, introduction by Gerry Kapolka, w/ silkscreen covers by Mat Daly. Printed in edition of 500, 2006. $20

HIP HOP APSARA by Anne Elizabeth Moore w/ color plates supplied by author and silkscreen covers by Angee Lennard. Printed in an edition of 500, 2012. $20

KORDIAN by Juliusz Słowacki, translated from Polish for the first time by Gerry Kapolka, w/ silkscreen covers by Aay Preston-Myint. Printed in edition of 500, 2011. $20

LOVE IS A CERTAIN FLOWER by Stephanie Brooks, w/ color plates supplied by author. Printed in edition of 250, 2009. $10

LUST & CASHMERE by A.E. Simns, w/ library card inserts by author, miniature hand-knit sweaters by Kellie Porter, and silkscreen covers by Alana Bailey. Winner of 2008 IPPY Independent Voice Award. Printed in edition of 500, 2007. $20

THE MUTATION OF FORTUNE by Erica Adams, w/ color plates supplied by author and silkscreen covers by Aay Preston-Myint. Printed in edition of 500, 2011. $20

THE NORTH GEORGIA GAZETTE reprint of original 1821 newspaper w/ excerpts from Captain Parry's log, and supplementary contemporary texts by John Huston and Lily Robert-Foley. Color plates by Daniel Anhorn, Deb Sokolow, Rebecca Mir and Jason Dunda, w/ silkscreen covers and limited edition 7" record provided by Nick Butcher. Printed in edition of 250, 2009. $30

ON MARVELLOUS THINGS HEARD by Gretchen E. Henderson, introduction by G.C. Waldrep, w/ color plates supplied by Carrie Gundersdorf. Printed in edition of 500, 2011. $12

PALM TREES by Nick Twemlow, introduction by Robert Fernandez, w/ 125 limited edition dust jackets silkscreened by Sonnenzimmer. Printed in an edition of 500, 2012. $15

A SEASON IN HELL by Arthur Rimbaud, translated by Nick Sarno, w/ color plates by Gerry Bacasa and cardstock silkscreen covers by Sonnenzimmer. Printed in edition of 500, 2009. $20

SERVICE MEDIA: IS IT "PUBLIC ART" OR IS IT ART IN PUBLIC SPACE? edited by Stuart Keeler, introduction by Carol Becker and silkscreen covers by Angee Leenard. Printed in and edition of 500, 2012. $20

SO MUCH BETTER by Terri Griffith, w/ color plate by Zoe Crosher and silkscreen covers by Nick Butcher of Sonnenzimmer. Nominated for 2009 Lambda Literary Prize. Printed in edition of 500, 2009. $20

TALKING WITH YOUR MOUTH FULL essays by Lori Waxman, Claire Pentecost & Carrie Lambert-Beattie, edited by Elizabeth Chodos. Printed in edition of 250, 2008. $10

URBESQUE A COLLECTION OF SHORT STORIES by Moshe Zvi Marvit, printed in edition of 500, w/ silkscreen covers by Mat Daly, 2006. $20

THE WHITE HOUSE by Joel Craig, introduction by John Beer, w/ 125 limited edition dust jackets silkscreened by Sonnenzimmer. Printed in an edition of 500, 2012. $15

WRITING ART CINEMA 1988–2010 by Stephen Lapthisophon, introduction by Devin King. Printed in an edition of 250, 2011. $10

↴ BOOKS PUBLISHED W/ THREEWALLS

ARTISTS RUN CHICAGO multiple contributors including Bad at Sports, Britton Bertran, Dan Gunn, Mary Jane Jacob, Allison Peters-Quinn, Temporary Services, and Lori Waxman. Printed in edition of 500, 2009. $20

PAPER & CARRIAGE VOLS. 1, 2 & 3, multiple contributors including Brooke Anderson, Dan Beachy-Quick, Jesse Ball, Elisa Bogos, Lilli Carré, Henry Darger, Daniel Johnston, Peter Orner, Mattathias Schwartz, and Kate Zambreno, w/ silkscreen covers by Dan MacAdam of Crosshair, Sean Stuckey, and Dan Wang. Vol 1 nominated for Utne Reader Award, Best New Publication. Printed in limited editions of 250, 2008. $18/ea.

THE PHONEBOOK VOL. 01 & 02, GUIDEBOOK edited by Caroline Picard, Nick Sarno, and Shannon Stratton. Printed in an edition of 500, 2006-2008. $10

NICK TWEMLOW lives with his family in Iowa City, where he writes and makes films. If you're interested in learning more, please visit nicktwemlow.com